SPACE TRAVEL

DR. MIKE GOLDSMITH

HODDER
Wayland

An imprint of Hodder Children's Books

SPACE TRAVEL

Other titles in the series: • Comets and Asteroids • Constellations • The Earth • The Moon • The Solar System • Space Mysteries • The Sun

© 2000 White-Thomson Publishing Ltd

Produced for Hodder Wayland by
White-Thomson Publishing Ltd
2/3 St. Andrew's Place
Lewes
East Sussex
BN7 1UP

Editor: Sarah Doughty
Designer: Tim Mayer
Consultant: Julia Hey, Jodrell Bank Science Centre

The right of Mike Goldsmith to be identified as the author of this Work has been asserted by him in accordance with the Copyright, Designs and Patents Act 1988.

A Catalogue record for this book is available from the British Library.

ISBN 0 7502 2724 9

Printed and bound in Italy by EuroGrafica, Vicenza

Published in Great Britain by Hodder Wayland, an imprint of Hodder Children's Books

Hodder Children's Books
a division of Hodder Headline Limited
338 Euston Road, London NW1 3BH

CONTENTS

ESCAPE FROM EARTH

The space mission was in trouble. There had been communications problems, the spaceship was going too fast, and now the alarm was buzzing, warning that the computer was overloaded.

The first story of a journey to the Moon was written about 160 AD. Instead of a rocket-powered spaceship, the Moon is reached by means of a sailing ship – and a very strong wind!

The spaceship was the *Eagle*, and its mission was to take American astronauts Neil Armstrong and Buzz Aldrin to the Moon, a place where no human had ever been.

Looking down at the landscape rushing by below, Armstrong saw that they were off course and heading straight towards a mass of boulders – if he didn't do something, their voyage would end with a spectacular crash.

◀ The *Eagle* approaches the Moon. The Earth is in view over the lunar horizon.

▲ Buzz Aldrin climbs down the ladder of the *Eagle* to become the second person (after Neil Armstrong) to set foot on the Moon.

The *Eagle* lands

Armstrong knew what he had to do: he took over control from the computer and diverted the spaceship's course. But the landing site he chose was covered in boulders too – and he had almost no fuel left. His next choice had to be his last: if it was wrong, he would die on the Moon, hundreds of thousands of kilometres from home. He changed the path of the spacecraft once more – and saw a clear space at last. With less than 30 seconds of fuel remaining, he eased the *Eagle* down to the Moon's surface, the rockets scattering dust that hadn't moved in a million years. The date was 20 July 1969, and people had landed on another world.

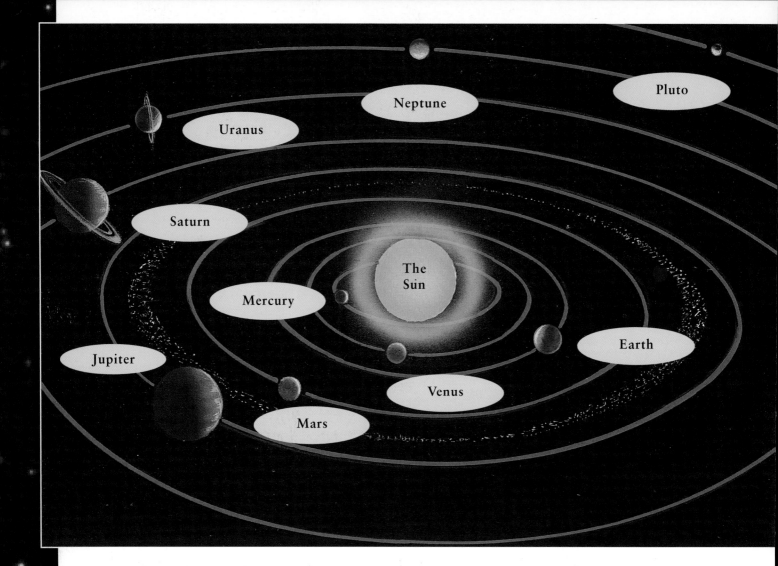

Pluto

Neptune

Uranus

Saturn

The Sun

Mercury

Earth

Jupiter

Venus

Mars

▲ The Sun and planets of the solar system (not to scale).

If the Sun suddenly exploded, we would not see it happen until the light reached the Earth, more than eight minutes later – until then we would still see the Sun shining normally in the sky.

The solar system

Space is vast. The nearest destination for a spacecraft is the Moon, which is over 350,000 km away. If there was a road to the Moon and a car drove along it at 100 km per hour, it would take more than four months to get there!

The rockets that took the astronauts to the Moon took just three days.

Space distances

Scientists sometimes measure the huge distances to planets or stars by the time light takes to get there. Light travels at the incredible speed of over a thousand million km per hour: it could go around the world seven times in one second.

A light second is the distance light travels in a second, or 300,000 km, and a light year is the distance light travels in a year, or 9.46 million million km.

Our neighbours	Closest Distance
The Moon	356,000 km (1.2 light seconds)
The planet Venus	38,000,000 km (2.1 light minutes)
The Sun	147,000,000 km (8.2 light minutes)
Proxima Centauri (the nearest star)	40,000,000,000,000 km (4.2 light years)

Although the distances to the other planets in the solar system are huge, spacecraft from Earth have visited all of them except Pluto. Some have now travelled thousands of millions of kilometres from Earth and are beyond the furthest planet and on their way to the stars.

◀ The *Voyager 2* space probe passing Neptune in 1989. The Sun can be seen 4.5 thousand million km (over 4 light-hours) away.

Rocket technology

Rockets work by burning fuel which releases a jet of gases to push the rocket forward. There are two types of fuel – solid and liquid.

Solid fuel rockets were invented in China hundreds of years ago and are still used as fireworks. But rockets that take people into space burn liquid fuels. All rocket fuel needs oxygen to burn. Because rockets have to travel through space where there is no oxygen, they take their own supply with them in liquid form.

The *Saturn V* had fuel tanks which were so well insulated that an ice cube placed in them would have taken eight years to melt!

▶ This *Saturn V* rocket, launched on 16 July 1969, resulted in the first manned lunar landing.

Rockets work quite differently to planes. A plane uses the air to help it fly, but a rocket is pushed forward by a jet of hot gases produced by burning fuel. Air just gets in the way of rockets – they move more easily in space. Most of the fuel of a rocket is used to escape from the pull of the Earth's gravity.

Once the rocket has reached a speed called the escape velocity, it is travelling fast enough to escape from the Earth without burning more fuel. The Earth's escape velocity is 11.2 km per second: hundreds of times faster than a firework rocket can travel.

The *Saturn V* rocket which took astronauts to the Moon burned almost 13 tonnes of fuel every second when it was launched.

The lighter a rocket is, the less fuel it needs. To reduce the weight of space rockets, sections are allowed to drop off once the fuel they contain has been used up. Rockets like these are called step-rockets.

▶ The *Saturn V* was a step-rocket over 110 m tall with the *Apollo* modules installed at the top.

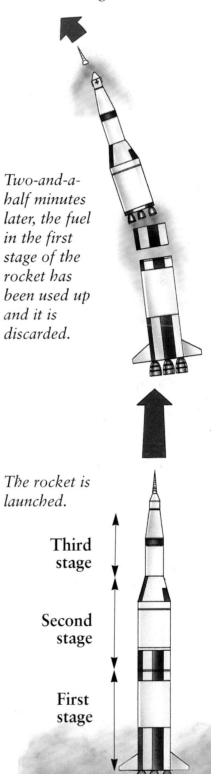

Eight-and-a-half minutes after launch, the second stage is discarded.

Two-and-a-half minutes later, the fuel in the first stage of the rocket has been used up and it is discarded.

The rocket is launched.

Third stage

Second stage

First stage

The first rockets

The liquid-fuel rocket was thought up in 1903 by a Russian scientist, Konstantin Tsiolkovsky, who also developed the theory of the step-rocket.

The first launch of a liquid-fuel rocket took place on 16 March 1926 from a farm in Massachusetts in the USA. The rocket wasn't very big, and it only reached a height of 12.5 m, but it marked a turning point in rocket history. Its inventor was Robert Goddard, an American physicist.

▲ The launch of one of Robert Goddard's rockets in 1937.

Bigger rockets called V2s were developed in Germany by Wernher von Braun during the Second World War. After the War, von Braun worked in America building space rockets.

In 1968, Russian tortoises flew round the Moon before returning safely to Earth in the *Zond 5* spaceship.

◀ The V2 was developed in Germany under the technical direction of von Braun. On its way to attack London in 1944, a V2 left the Earth's atmosphere and became the first spaceship.

The first satellites

In October 1957, people all over the world tuned in to hear a strange beeping sound from their radios. The signals came from a satellite called *Sputnik 1* which Russia had launched into space. The space age had begun. The next year, the *Juno 1* rocket put *Explorer 1*, America's first satellite, into orbit. *Explorer 1* discovered that near the Earth there are regions filled with radiation that would be deadly to unprotected space travellers. These are called Van Allen belts and are formed by the Earth's magnetism, which traps particles from the Sun.

▲ The first satellite, *Sputnik 1*, which was launched in 1957.

Thousands of satellites are now in orbit around the Earth. They do all sorts of jobs, from monitoring the weather to relaying television programmes.

The first space travellers

Soon after *Sputnik 1*, the Russians sent the first traveller into orbit – a dog called Laika, on *Sputnik 2*. The Americans soon sent animals into space too, including a chimpanzee called Ham. These animal astronauts showed that it would be possible for people to survive space travel.

▲ Space-travelling chimpanzee Ham accepts an apple soon after returning to Earth.

SPACE PEOPLE

Orbiting the Earth

In 1961, a 27 year-old Russian pilot called Yuri Gagarin made history by escaping from the Earth's atmosphere and becoming the first human space traveller. He orbited the Earth once before returning home. He was soon followed by others. Valentina Tereshkova became the first woman in space in 1963. Alexei Leonov was the first person to leave his spacecraft and walk in space – protected by a spacesuit.

▲ Russian space-traveller Yuri Gagarin, the first person to travel in space.

The first American astronaut to be blasted into space was Alan Shepard, in 1961, who spent just 15 minutes in space before dropping down into the Atlantic Ocean. The next year, astronaut John Glenn was launched into space and made three orbits of the Earth in less than five hours.

◀ American astronaut, John Glenn, boards his *Mercury* spaceship in 1962.

When their *Voskhod 2* spaceship returned to Earth 3,000 km off course in 1965, and landed in a forest, Russian astronauts had to cope with a pack of hungry wolves.

Journeys to the Moon

When rockets became powerful enough to break away from the Earth's gravity, the Moon became the next goal of space exploration. In 1961, the USA committed itself to landing a person on the Moon by 1970.

In 1965 and 1966, ten manned *Gemini* spacecraft were launched, to get astronauts ready for Moon journeys. The astronauts practised space walking and found out how living in space affected them. They learnt how to fly spaceships, and even how to join them together in space.

◀ Buzz Aldrin leaves *Gemini 12,* as part of his training for a landing on the Moon.

LIVING IN SPACE

Valerij Poliyakov spent a record 437 days aboard the *Mir* space station.

▼ Astronauts in the airlock of the *Discovery* space shuttle, on its way to the Russian space station *Mir* in 1995.

Life in space is difficult and dangerous. There is no air to breathe, so spacecraft have to take their own supplies with them. The lack of air also means that special protection is needed from the deadly radiation of the Sun and that any places that are in shadow are bitterly cold.

Astronauts can only leave their spacecraft wearing spacesuits to protect them from the airlessness, radiation and extreme temperatures in space.

In modern spacecraft, all these problems have been overcome, but there is one thing that astronauts still have to cope with – weightlessness. In space, there is no up or down, and people and things float. You can't drink a cup of tea in space because the tea would just float out of the cup – you have to suck it through a straw instead.

▲ In the weightless environment of the *Mir* space station, crew members of two spacecraft meet.

Weightlessness causes all sorts of changes in people: they can grow several centimetres taller, and, unless they do special exercises, their muscles shrink and their bones weaken. Many space travellers also suffer from space sickness, which is like air sickness but which luckily soon wears off.

The longest space walk took 8 hours and 29 minutes. It happened in 1992, when shuttle astronauts had to grapple with a faulty satellite.

FROM THE EARTH TO THE MOON

When the exploration of space began, Russia and America were fierce rivals, and each tried to out-do the other. In particular, they were both keen to win the space race to the Moon.

Many people thought the Russians would win. In 1959, they managed to put the first piece of Earth equipment on the Moon when they crashed a rocket called *Luna 2* there.

In the same year, *Luna 3* flew behind the Moon, and a photograph was taken of something that no one had ever seen – the Moon's far side, which is never turned towards the Earth.

▲ The far side of the Moon, which cannot be seen from Earth.

The astronauts who travelled in *Apollo 10* to go around the Moon broke all human speed records: they travelled at 39,897 km per hour – more than 33 times the speed of sound.

More unmanned explorations followed, by both US and Russian spacecraft. A series of US *Ranger* spacecraft sent back spectacular close-ups of the lunar surface before they crashed onto it, but the Russian *Luna 9* was the first craft to land safely on the Moon, and *Luna 10* – also Russian – was the first to orbit it. But in the end, the Americans won the race to be first to land people there.

Teflon is a material that was developed to stop moving parts of spacecraft from sticking together – but it was soon used on Earth too, to make non-stick pans.

Neil Armstrong and Buzz Aldrin stepped out of the *Eagle* in 1969 to become the first people to set foot on the Moon. The footprints they made will probably still be there millions of years in the future.

◀ Buzz Aldrin standing on the Moon's surface in 1969. Reflected in his vizor, Neil Armstrong and the *Eagle* can be seen.

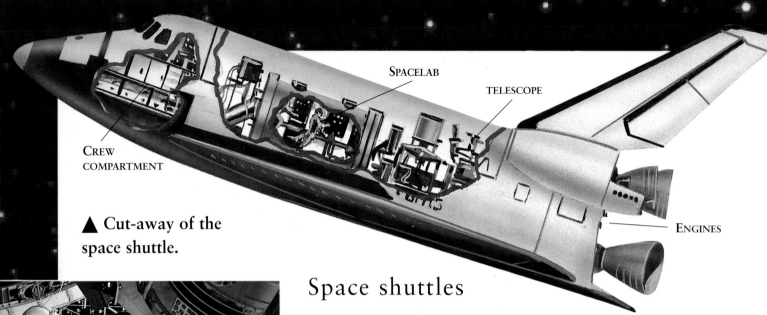

SPACELAB

TELESCOPE

CREW COMPARTMENT

ENGINES

▲ Cut-away of the space shuttle.

Space shuttles

The rockets that took people to the Moon were enormous – and very expensive. And they could only be used once. Something cheaper was needed that could be used over and over again, so, in the 1970s, the USA built the first space shuttle. Space shuttles are now used regularly, to launch and repair satellites, for military missions and for scientific work. But there have been problems too – in 1986 the shuttle *Challenger* exploded soon after take-off due to a gas leak and the whole crew of seven died.

Space stations

In 1971 a new satellite called *Salyut 1* was sent into space – but this one was different, because people could live in it.

▲ A full-size model of the Russian *Salyut 1* space station.

Two spiders became famous in 1973 when they learnt to build webs in the weightless environment of the *Skylab* space station. Their first attempts were a mess, but they got much better with practice.

Satellites with people on board are called space stations: the first US space station was *Skylab* which was launched in 1973 and stayed in space until 1979, when it crashed back to Earth.

In 1869, a magazine published the first story about a space station – made of bricks! The story was *The Brick Moon* by E. E Hale.

The Russian space station *Mir* was launched in 1986 and was in use for over ten years. A new International Space Station is being built in orbit around the Earth – a joint venture between the USA, Japan, Canada, Europe and Russia. The structure will have six laboratories and living accommodation.

▼ The International Space Station will be powered by 4,000 sq m of solar panels and will accommodate six crew members at a time.

SPACE MISSIONS

Sending people into space is very expensive, because of all the life-support equipment that needs to go with them. So there have been no manned Moon landings since 1972, and the space-probes that have travelled beyond the Moon have not had people on board.

Each rocket that took astronauts to the Moon burned up enough fuel to fill an Olympic swimming pool. But once a spacecraft is on its way and has escaped from the Earth's gravity, it will keep on going until it either crashes into something, or is pulled down by the gravity of another planet. This is because, in space, there is no air to slow down the spaceship.

▲ The giant planet Neptune, photographed by the *Voyager 2* probe in 1989. A storm system, called the Great Dark Spot, can be seen on the left, with bright white clouds nearby.

The theory of gravitation was used to find the planet Neptune in 1846. Astronomers noticed that Uranus was not moving through space quite as they expected. They thought that the gravitational pull of an unkown planet might be responsible, and found Neptune where they predicted it should be.

► The 'slingshot' effect was used by *Voyager 2* to explore the outer solar system. By passing close to Jupiter, the space-probe used the gravity of the giant planet to increase its speed and steer it towards Saturn, Uranus and Neptune.

When the slingshot effect is used to speed up a spacecraft, the planet slows down – by an amount less than a millionth of a millionth of a millimetre per second!

By steering a spacecraft near a planet, it is possible to use the planet's gravity to help speed it up. This is called the 'slingshot' effect. There was a big piece of luck for space explorers in the 1970s. They realized that the four giant planets Jupiter, Saturn, Uranus and Neptune would soon be lined up. This meant it was possible to use the 'slingshot' effect to send spacecraft such as *Pioneer* and *Voyager* on 'grand tours' to see them all. Alignments like this only happen every 180 years.

EXPLORING THE PLANETS

Unmanned space probes have led the way in the exploration of the solar system.

Venus

The first successful probe to another planet was *Mariner 2*, which flew past the planet Venus in 1962. Space probes which venture inside the atmosphere of Venus are soon melted and crushed by the intense heat and pressure, but some have managed to land and send back photographs of the surface before they were destroyed.

Mars

Mariner 4 flew past Mars in 1965, taking photographs which showed that Mars had a Moon-like surface. In 1976, two American *Viking* craft landed there and sent back pictures of the rocky landscape.

Mariner 1 was a probe that was supposed to go to Venus. It went off course and had to be destroyed – because a dash had been left out of its computer's coded instructions!

▲ Mars, photographed by the *Viking 1* spacecraft. The giant volcano Olympus is visible at top right, and three more volcanoes can be seen centre right.

In 1997, the *Pathfinder* mission carried a small robot rover to Mars to travel across the rough surface of the planet.

Mercury

In 1974, *Mariner 10* flew past Mercury, the closest planet to the Sun, and sent back the first images of its surface – which was covered in craters like those on the Moon.

The outer planets

In the 1970s, *Pioneer 10*, *Pioneer 11*, *Voyager 1* and *Voyager 2* were launched on missions to visit the outer planets (Jupiter, Saturn, Uranus and Neptune) and their moons. The *Galileo* probe later visited Jupiter, venturing inside the thick atmosphere of the planet for the first time.

Pictures and video discs are included in several space probes, as messages to any aliens they may encounter.

◀ *Pioneer 10* reaches Jupiter in 1973. The intense radiation from the planet almost destroyed the space probe's instruments.

FUTURE VOYAGES

Saturn

▼ The *Cassini* spacecraft approaches Titan. The dish-shaped object on the left is the *Huygens* probe.

In 1997, the American *Cassini* spacecraft set off on a journey to Saturn, to arrive there in 2004. As well as photographing the giant planet, its rings and its moons, *Cassini* carried a European probe, called *Huygens,* which will parachute down through the atmosphere of Titan, Saturn's biggest moon.

Mars

For a manned mission to Mars, a whole series of spaceships is planned. The first craft will carry supplies and equipment for the human explorers who will arrive later, after travelling through space for at least four months.

Saturn's moon, Titan, is the only one in the solar system with a thick atmosphere. It contains chemicals like those found in fumes from car exhausts.

On Mars, things weigh only a third as much as they do on Earth, years are nearly twice as long, and the sky is pink.

Once they are there, they will probably stay for over a year, looking for hidden water supplies, searching for traces of life – and making their own fuel, oxygen and water from material found on Mars itself. This mission will be extremely expensive, and no date for it has yet been set.

Pluto and beyond

Pluto, the outermost planet in the solar system, is the only one never to have been visited, but there are plans to send a probe there – which might arrive in 2012. The probe would also investigate Pluto's moon, Charon, and might be sent on beyond Pluto to explore some mysterious icy objects that have recently been discovered far out in space.

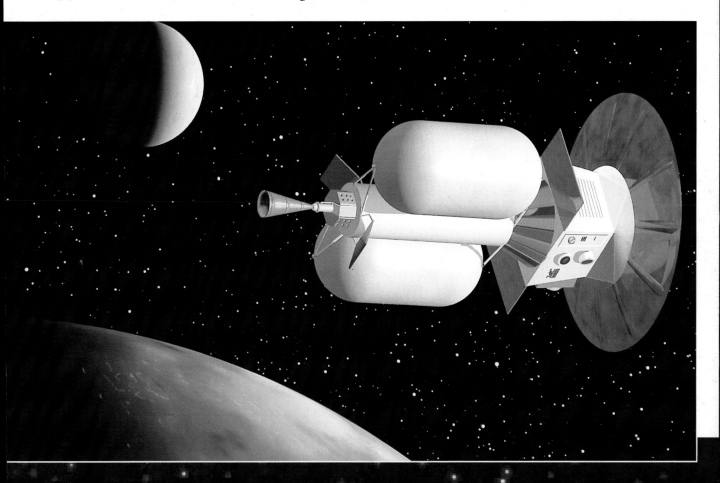

▼ The proposed Pluto-Kuiper Express space probe near the planet Pluto. Pluto's huge moon, Charon, can be seen in the upper left of the picture.

SPACESHIPS OF TOMORROW

So far, spaceships have been powered by rockets which burn liquid fuels, sometimes helped by gravity. But liquid fuels are heavy and expensive, and gravity can only be used for certain routes through the solar system. So tomorrow's spaceships will need to find other sources of power.

In the 1950s, a spaceship was suggested that would work by exploding atomic bombs behind it – at a rate of 5 per second!

The solar sail

There are plans for a spaceship that won't need to carry its own fuel – it will use the power of the Sun instead. The spaceship is called a solar sail because the pressure of the Sun's light pushes it through space as the wind pushes a sailing ship through the sea.

▶ A solar sail drifting above the Earth.

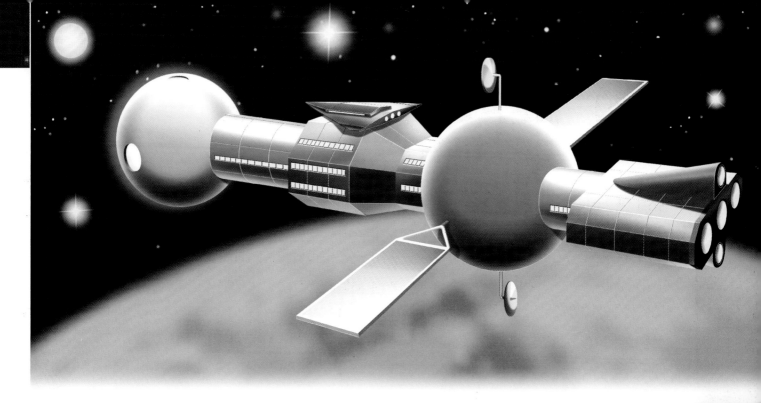

▲ A possible antimatter spaceship of the future, equipped with a shuttle craft to ferry its passengers to the planets it visits. The glow at the front is an energy-field used to protect it from meteoroids on its long journeys.

Ion drive

Ion drives have already been used to manoeuvre some satellites. In an ion-drive engine, oxygen or other substances are broken down into fragments, called ions, which are charged with electricity. Electromagnets are then used to fire these ions into space – the ions push the spacecraft forward instead of the burning gases that rockets use.

Antimatter

If a piece of antimatter the size of a grain of sand was allowed to touch ordinary matter, enough energy would be released to boil more than 10 million kettles.

Antimatter is a substance which looks just like ordinary matter. But, when antimatter and normal matter touch, they destroy each other and an enormous amount of energy is released. Tiny amounts of antimatter are made on Earth even now, and it may one day be possible to use it to power spacecraft.

STARSHIPS

In the distant future, it may be possible for people to travel to other stars.

▼ A possible human colony on another planet. The thin, unbreathable atmosphere means that the colony would have to be protected by a pressurized dome.

The Earth will not last forever. In millions of years time, the Sun will grow so big that the Earth will either be swallowed up or get so hot that everything on it will be destroyed. Escape to other star-systems would need new types of engines. Even then, the journeys are likely to take many years – even centuries!

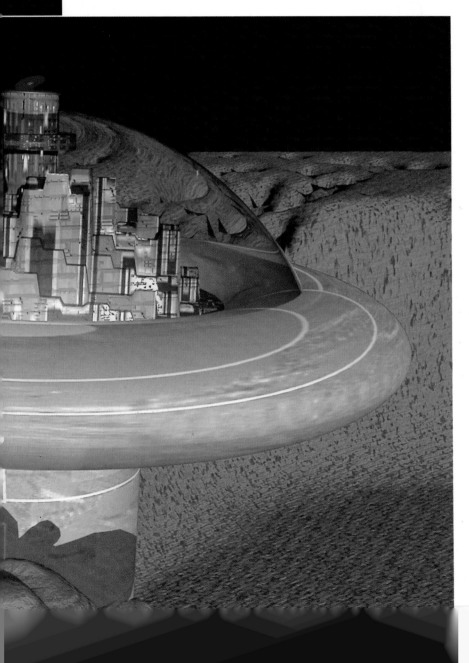

Many planets orbiting other stars have been found and more are being discovered each year. So if we ever manage to reach the stars, there will be many new worlds to explore.

▲ A gigantic spaceship of the distant future, capable of crossing the enormous spaces between the stars.

The *Voyager* and *Pioneer* space probes should eventually reach other stars – after journeys lasting more than 80,000 years.

To survive such long journeys through space, people might be put into a deep sleep for a long time by making them very cold. Experiments on animals have shown that this is possible. Automatic systems would wake the space travellers up again, perhaps hundreds of years later. By then, they would be millions and millions of kilometres from Earth.

People who travel so far would never return to Earth, but they might set up colonies on planets going round other stars, far away in space and time.

GLOSSARY

Antimatter Possible fuel for future spaceships. Pure energy can be converted to equal amounts of matter and antimatter.

Astronaut A person who travels through space.

Atmosphere Layer of gases surrounding the Earth or other planet or moon.

Escape velocity The speed a spaceship must reach to escape from a planet.

Gravity The pull that holds us to Earth and keeps the planets going round the Sun.

Ion drive A device which uses a stream of broken-up atoms to push a spacecraft through space.

Light year The distance that light travels in a year – 9.46 million million kilometres.

Lunar To do with the Moon.

Meteoroids Solid objects, often the remains of comets, that travel through space.

NASA The National Aeronautics and Space Administration, which organizes space exploration on behalf of the US government.

Orbit The path of one object around another.

Satellite An orbiting body: either a moon or an artificial object.

Solar To do with the Sun.

Solar sail A device which uses the power of the Sun to push it through space.

Solar system The Sun and the planets, asteroids and comets that go round it.

Space probe An unmanned spacecraft sent to explore space.

Space shuttle A reusable spacecraft which carries people and material into space. It is launched by a rocket but lands like a plane.

Space sickness Illness which affects many space-travellers.

Space station An artificial satellite which can carry people.

FURTHER INFORMATION

Web pages:

www.nasa.gov NASA website

www.esrin.esa.it European Space Agency website

www.iki.rssi.ru Russian Space Agency website

nssdc.gsfc.nasa.gov History of all space missions

Books to read:

Amazing Pop-Up Space Shuttle by David Hawcock (Dorling Kindersley, 1998)

The History News: in Space by Michael Johnstone & Douglas Millard (Walker Books, 1999)

How to Get to the Moon by Hazel Richardson (Oxford Books, 1999)

Moon Landing by Carole Stott (Dorling Kindersley, 1999)

The Science Museum book of Amazing Facts: Space by Anthony Wilson (Hodder Children's Books, 1996)

Superscientists series: The Cosmic Professor, Heaven's Above, The Colour of Light (Hodder Wayland, 1998)

CD-ROM

Interfact Space Travel (Two-Can, 1999)

Places to visit:

Jodrell Bank Science Centre, Macclesfield, Cheshire, SK11 9DL (Tel: 01477 571339).

The Planetarium, Euston Road, London (Tel: 0207 935 6861) has shows which feature stars and planets.

The Science Museum, Exhibition Road, South Kensington, London (Tel: 0207 938 8000) includes lots of astronomy exhibits.

The Royal Observatory Greenwich, London (Tel: 0208 312 6557) includes historical telescopes and has a planetarium.

ART AND CRAFT
- Make a model of the *Eagle* on the Moon.
- Look at pictures of spaceships to see how their design has changed, and then draw a picture of your idea of a future spaceship.

TECHNOLOGY
- Work out the properties of the materials that would be needed to build a spacecraft.
- Design a space station where you could live and work comfortably.

ENGLISH
- Imagine you have travelled to the Moon with Armstrong and Aldrin. Write an article about the journey.
- Read science-fiction stories about space exploration.

SPACE TRAVEL

MATHS
- If it takes a spacecraft three days to travel from the Earth to the Moon, work out how long it would take to get to Venus. What assumptions do you need to make to do this?
- Work out how much you would weigh on the Moon.

HISTORY
- Find out about the stories and legends surrounding the planets.
- Find out about the rocket scientists: Tsiolkovsky, Goddard, Winkler, Oberth, von Braun, Korolev, Tsander.

SCIENCE
- Experiment with different ways of propelling model spacecraft using catapults or balloons.

INDEX

All numbers in **bold** refer to pictures.

Picture acknowledgements:

The publishers would like to thank the following for allowing their pictures to be reproduced in this book: Bruce Coleman/Astrofoto 8, 16, 29; Eye Ubiquitous *cover*; HWPL 10 (top); Science Photo Library *cover*, 25/David Ducros 24/Victor Habbick 28/David A Hardy 11 (top), 21/Seth Shostak 7/NASA 14, 19, 20, 22; Popperfoto 4, 5, 10 (bottom), 11 (bottom), 12 (both), 13, 15, 17, 18; Peter Bull Art Studio 2, 26, 27; all other artwork from HWPL.